Original title:

A Quiet Frost

Copyright © 2024 Swan Charm
All rights reserved.

Author: Paulina Pähkel
ISBN HARDBACK: 978-9916-79-918-5
ISBN PAPERBACK: 978-9916-79-919-2
ISBN EBOOK: 978-9916-79-920-8

Cool Respite in the Breath of Winter

The chill creeps in, a soft embrace,
Breathe in the frost, this quiet place.
Snowflakes dance on the gentle breeze,
Whispering secrets among the trees.

Icicles form like glittering tears,
Time slows down, erasing fears.
Nights stretch long under starry gleam,
Wrapped in warmth, lost in a dream.

Where the World Pauses in White

Blankets of snow, a peaceful sight,
Hushed whispers echo through the night.
Footsteps crunch on the frosted floor,
Every breath a soft, silent score.

The twilight glows with a silver hue,
Nature rests, wrapped in a shroud so new.
As time stands still in pristine light,
A world transformed, pure and bright.

The Peace of Crystal-Covered Ground

Leaves of frost adorn the earth,
In this cold, we find rebirth.
Each step a symphony of sound,
Wrapped in peace, we are spellbound.

Beneath the weight of winter's crown,
Silence reigns without a frown.
The world is hushed, a soothing balm,
In crystal fields, we find our calm.

In the Grip of Still Night's Whisper

Stars above in a velvet sky,
Softly twinkling, they seem to sigh.
Moonlight spills on the frozen ground,
In the stillness, our hearts are found.

Night wraps us in its tender hold,
Stories shared that never grow old.
In the silence, dreams take flight,
In the grip of still, sweet night.

The Graceful Pause of Nature's Cycle

In the hush where whispers tread,
Leaves descend like dreams unsaid,
Time holds still, a moment rare,
An autumn breath, soft in the air.

Beneath the sky, the clouds exhale,
A symphony, both grand and frail,
Golden hues, the sun's last glance,
Nature sways in quiet dance.

Rivers mirror the fading light,
Echoes of day yield to night,
In this pause, life softly glows,
The silent world, as beauty flows.

Stars awaken in shimmering grace,
Their twinkle paints the cosmic space,
While crickets sing in lingering calls,
Time weaves magic, as night falls.

Rest in this moment, nature's art,
Embrace the stillness, let it start,
For in the pause, the heart can find,
The cycle of life, entwined and kind.

Gentle Echoes of Chilled Whimsy

In the air, a crisp delight,
Whispers dance in frosty flight,
Laughter mingles with the chill,
Winter's charm, the heart to fill.

Footprints left on powdered white,
Stories shared beneath moonlight,
Breezes weave through trees up high,
Nature's lullaby, soft sigh.

Snowflakes twirl in errant play,
Wrapping dreams in snowy sway,
Each a tale from skies above,
A gentle whisper, purest love.

Fires crackle, warmth embraced,
In this peace, our worries chased,
Cocoa sipped by amber glow,
Together here, our spirits flow.

With each heartbeat, winter's grace,
Echoes linger, softly trace,
In chilled whimsy, life's embrace,
We find our joy in every space.

The Quietude of a Frozen World

Snowflakes drift in silence,
Blanketing the earth below.
Whispers of the winter winds,
Embrace the chill that doesn't go.

Trees stand tall, ageless sentinels,
Caught in a tranquil winter's dream.
Stillness wraps the world in peace,
Frozen beauty, soft and supreme.

Footprints echo in the snow,
Marking journeys only few dare take.
Each step a gentle cadence,
In a land where all is awake.

Icicles glimmer, sharp and clear,
Catching light from the pale sun.
Nature pauses, holding its breath,
In a frozen state, all is one.

The quietude, a soothing balm,
Softens hearts, brings clarity.
In this world of white enchantment,
We find our own serenity.

Stillness in the Glistening Pines

Pines adorned with sparkling frost,
Stand like guardians of the night.
Whispers linger in the air,
Underneath the silver light.

Softly falls the evening hush,
As shadows lengthen, stretch and yawn.
Heartbeat calms within the woods,
As the stars begin to dawn.

Moonlight dances on the branches,
Crafting patterns, rich and bold.
In this sanctuary of stillness,
Stories of the night unfold.

Frozen scents of earth and pine,
Merge with whispers of the breeze.
Time stands still in this moment,
Nature speaks, our hearts at ease.

Breathless silence drapes the night,
In the warmth of winter's glow.
Here beneath the glistening pines,
Life moves gently, soft and slow.

Ethereal Glow of a Winter's Night

Underneath a darkened sky,
Stars spread forth like scattered dreams.
The world transforms, ethereal glow,
As winter's silent beauty gleams.

Crystalline forms grace the ground,
Shimmering in the moon's embrace.
Nights of magic and wonder loom,
In the stillness, a gentle grace.

Frost cloaks branches, elegant veils,
Each sparkle holds a whispered tune.
Softly breathe the darkest hours,
Touched by light of a winter's moon.

Voices of the night conversing,
In melodies the heart can feel.
Nature's slumber, pure and calm,
Wrapped in warmth, a peaceful seal.

As dawn creeps in with softest light,
The glow will fade, yet not remain.
Memories linger from the night,
Ethereal and free from pain.

Hushed Conversations with the Stars

Above a world draped in white,
Stars twinkle in the deep blue dark.
Each flicker holds a secret truth,
A celestial song, a cosmic spark.

In the quiet of the night,
Whispers linger in the air.
Conversations of the universe,
Echo softly, everywhere.

Constellations weave their tales,
In patterns only few can see.
Guiding hearts like ancient mariners,
Across the silent, tranquil sea.

In this realm of endless space,
Dreams take flight on silver wings.
Hushed confessions shared with light,
The song of winter softly sings.

So pause to gaze, to listen close,
To the stories written in the sky.
In the stillness, find your peace,
Amidst the stars, we learn to fly.

Still Waters Under a Whispering Sky

The calm reflects the fading light,
A gentle breeze begins to sigh.
Whispers dance along the shore,
As stars awaken, one by one.

Moonlight glimmers on the glass,
Rippling softly, shadows pass.
Nature hums a tranquil tune,
In harmony with dusk and noon.

Silence reigns in soft embrace,
While dreams take flight, they find their place.
The world holds breath, as time drifts slow,
In stillness where the spirits flow.

Every ripple tells a tale,
Of journeys lost and hearts that sail.
Underneath the sighing trees,
Life unfolds upon the breeze.

Gentle Haze of the Morning Chill

A soft embrace of misty air,
Lingers lightly everywhere.
Leaves are kissed by dew's cool hand,
Nature wakes across the land.

Sunlight peeks, a tender glow,
Painting hills with warmth, so slow.
The horizon blushes bright,
As day embraces the fading night.

Birds begin their sweet refrain,
A symphony of joy and pain.
Every note a fresh delight,
In the gentle morning light.

Whispers of the world awake,
In each breath that nature takes.
Time slows down in morning's chill,
A tranquil heart, a placid will.

A Silent Canvas of White

The world is wrapped in winter's grace,
A silent canvas, an empty space.
Each flake falls with a dancer's poise,
In the hush where nature enjoys.

Snow-capped trees, a soft display,
Whispers linger where children play.
Footsteps crunch in the fresh, pure snow,
A trail of magic only we know.

Twilight glows, the sky feels wide,
As silent lands stretch far and wide.
The world transformed by winter's gleam,
A frozen landscape feels like a dream.

Time stands still, the air is clear,
Every breath drawn, a promise near.
In this stillness, we find our breath,
In the embrace of winter's depth.

The Soft Murmur of Snowflakes

Falling gently, a whispered song,
Snowflakes tumble, drift along.
Each one unique, a fragile grace,
Kissing the earth, a soft embrace.

The world shimmers in twilight's glow,
Where silence reigns, and dreams can flow.
Hushed are the voices, muted and low,
In the embrace of the soft white snow.

Nature's touch, so pure and bright,
Brings forth beauty in the night.
The soft murmur carries on,
As winter weaves its quiet song.

Moments linger in the chill,
Hearts are warmed, yet time stands still.
Wrapped in peace, a perfect night,
Under the stars, everything feels right.

Traces of Silence in the Cold

In the winter's breath it lies,
Frosted air, a hush, a sigh.
Footsteps fade on icy ground,
Echoes lost, no sound around.

Bare trees shiver, holding still,
Moonlight paints a silhouette thrill.
Stars twinkle like quiet dreams,
In the dark, nothing redeems.

Shadows dance in crystal light,
Whispers of the coming night.
Nature holds its breath in peace,
In this moment, all can cease.

Silence weaves a gentle thread,
Through the places spirits tread.
Time stands still beneath the sky,
In the cold where echoes lie.

Fragments of Serenity in White

Softly falls the snow so bright,
Cloaking all in purest white.
Each flake a piece of silent grace,
In this calm, a warm embrace.

Gentle hush, the world slows down,
Nature wears a crystal crown.
Footsteps mark the quiet ground,
In this stillness, peace is found.

Branches bow with heavy coats,
Carrying secrets, nature's notes.
Underneath the blanket sleeps,
A world where harmony keeps.

Moments linger, softly spun,
In the glow of setting sun.
The night will cradle dreams tonight,
In the joy of frigid white.

Tenderness in the Skeletal Branches

Naked trees against the sky,
Hold the whispers, secrets shy.
Gnarled fingers reach for light,
Tenderness in winter's bite.

Every branch, a story told,
In the chill, a heart so bold.
They stand firm through storm and cold,
Emblems of the life they hold.

Graceful lines in muted tone,
Frame the dusk where shadows moan.
Each crack and crevice marks the year,
Winter's breath, a touch so dear.

Silence lingers, peace bestows,
In the stillness, life still grows.
Underneath the frost and snow,
Tender hearts in silence glow.

The Whispering Cold of Dusk

As dusk descends, the cold persists,
Whispers carried on the mists.
Sky bleeds shades of twilight gray,
Nature pauses, holding sway.

Chill wraps around the fading light,
As day embraces coming night.
Stars emerge, a gentle spark,
In the air, a soft remark.

In the hush, the world exhales,
Fading sounds like distant sails.
The chill cradles every breath,
Yet, within lies warmth, not death.

Silhouettes in fading hues,
Home awaits with tender views.
As night unfolds its velvet cloak,
The heart converses, soft and woke.

Quietude Beneath a White Canvas

In the stillness of the morn,
Snowflakes dance, soft and warm.
Whispers drift through frosty air,
Nature's hush, beyond compare.

Blankets white on sleeping ground,
Tranquil sights, no harsh sounds.
Footprints fade with each soft tread,
Silent stories left unsaid.

Branches bare, their secrets kept,
Underneath where shadows crept.
A canvas pure, so vast and wide,
Where winter's dreams quietly bide.

Time slows down, the world unwinds,
In the peace, the heart aligns.
Softly now the moments flow,
In quietude, I let go.

Frosted Memories Beneath the Stars

Underneath the starry night,
Frosted glimmers, pure delight.
Whispers of a past long gone,
Echo softly as dawn draws on.

Frozen laughs beneath the moon,
In this chill, we hum our tune.
Memories twirl like falling snow,
Dancing softly, ever slow.

Beneath blankets of glistening light,
Shadows flicker, taking flight.
Each crystal holds a whispered tale,
Of love and loss, in winter's veil.

Stars reflect in icy streams,
Every twinkle, holding dreams.
Once again, we find our way,
Through the frost of yesterday.

Dreams Suspended in Ice

In the silence, dreams reside,
Encased in ice, a secret guide.
Frozen wishes, glimmer bright,
Shining softly in the night.

Thoughts like snowflakes drift and glide,
Through a world where hopes abide.
Each crystal holds a flickering spark,
Illuminating shadows stark.

Suspended high, like stars in skies,
Silent echoes, whispered sighs.
Capture moments, time's embrace,
In frozen realms, we find our place.

Time stands still, the world awaits,
While dreams gather at icy gates.
Through the chill, our spirits soar,
In this stillness, we explore.

Gentle Crystals on the Lawn

Morning breaks with silver light,
Crystals twinkle, soft and bright.
On the lawn where children play,
Nature's jewels greet the day.

Gentle whispers on the breeze,
Rustling leaves, the dancing trees.
Each step taken, careful, slow,
Tracing patterns in the snow.

Dewdrops cling to blades of green,
A delicate, enchanting scene.
In the sunlight, colors blend,
Nature's art, without an end.

Smiles exchanged, laughter sounds,
Joyful echoes cross the grounds.
In every crystal, life is spun,
On the lawn, we all are one.

The Promise of Warmth in Chill

In the heart of winter's sail,
The sun whispers through the pale.
Each beam a promise, soft and clear,
Chasing away the cloak of fear.

Beneath the frost, life starts to stir,
With dreams of blooms that soon occur.
A gentle hope begins to rise,
As hues of spring light up the skies.

While chilly winds weave tales of old,
The warmth within begins to mold.
Each breath of life, a spark of fire,
Igniting hearts with pure desire.

The promise lingers in the air,
A touch of warmth beyond compare.
With every dawn that breaks anew,
A symphony of green ensues.

Ethereal Silence of Frost's Embrace

In the stillness, frost will cling,
To branches bare, a jeweled ring.
Each crystal spark, a silent song,
In winter's hush, where dreams belong.

Nature holds her breath so tight,
In the calm of soft moonlight.
Stars reflect on ice so bright,
A world transformed, serene and white.

Whispers dance on chilly air,
Secrets shared with not a care.
The night's embrace, a velvet shroud,
Where silence reigns and peace is loud.

Ethereal like the falling snow,
Time stands still, the world aglow.
In this quiet, hearts find grace,
In frost's embrace, a warm embrace.

Melodies of the Icy Silence

Beneath the veil of winter's breath,
Lies the song of silent death.
Each note a chill, a fleeting sound,
As icebound whispers wrap around.

The trees sway gently, clad in white,
Their voices muted, pale and slight.
Chimes of frost in the midnight air,
Compose a tune beyond compare.

Nature's heart beats soft and low,
In frozen realms where shadows flow.
The harmony of cold's embrace,
Leaves a trace of quiet grace.

In icy silence, melodies rise,
Echoing softly beneath the skies.
Each breath of winter, a fleeting sigh,
As stars blink bright in the frosty sky.

Icy Breath of the Sleeping Earth

The earth beneath is fast asleep,
In icy layers, secrets keep.
A breath so cold, it stills the night,
While dreams entwine in silver light.

The ground, a quilt of frosty whites,
Holds echoes of the summer's flights.
In whispered tones, the soil sighs,
Awaiting warmth 'neath azure skies.

Each chill that sweeps across the land,
Brings forth the touch of winter's hand.
A sacred bond of peace and rest,
In frozen realms, the earth is blessed.

The icy breath, a lullaby,
Cradles life with a gentle sigh.
Beneath the frost, a promise grows,
For spring will come, as nature knows.

Ephemeral Art on Windowpanes

Frosted patterns dance and sway,
Nature's brush strokes fade away.
A fleeting glimpse of winter's charm,
In icy whispers, soft and warm.

Each dawn unveils a new display,
A tapestry that won't stay.
Colors merge, then disappear,
A moment's beauty, crystal clear.

The sun breaks forth, the canvas glows,
As melting art, the silence goes.
Yet in its wake, we find delight,
In memories of that frozen sight.

Oh, seasonal dance, a joyous waltz,
In winter's grip, we find no faults.
A vibrant life in coldest night,
Ephemeral, but pure, and bright.

Sleepy Silence Wrapped in Crystal

Snowflakes fall, a gentle hush,
Cloaked in stillness, world in blush.
Whispers float on frosty air,
Nature rests, devoid of care.

Each branch adorned with icy lace,
In shadowed woods, a sacred space.
Dreams drift softly on the ground,
In peaceful slumber, life is found.

Time stands still, as moments freeze,
Wrapped in wonder, hearts appease.
The dawn unfolds, a tender breath,
Crystalline spells weave life from death.

In twilight's glow, we seek the light,
A tranquil warmth beneath the night.
Sleepy silence, in layers steep,
Cradles us in dreams so deep.

Beneath the Weight of Winter's Breath

Heavy hangs the morning chill,
Winter's sigh, so deep and still.
Each crystal breath that nature takes,
A breath of life, warm heart awakes.

Blankets of white, a soft embrace,
Hides the earth in frigid grace.
Branches bow to burdens vast,
Yet beauty blooms, though shadows cast.

Underneath the weight, we thrive,
In colder nights, our dreams survive.
Together we find warmth inside,
In winter's clutch, we will abide.

The world transforms, a silent plea,
In frosty confines, we seek to be.
Beneath each breath, a story spun,
Of life renewed when winter's done.

Frost-Covered Secrets of the Night

Moonlight drapes the world in sheen,
Frost-covered secrets, hushed and keen.
Each shimmer tells of hidden lore,
In whispers soft, we seek the more.

Valleys deep and mountain high,
Crystals glisten, twinkling sly.
Guarded tales in frozen air,
Silent moonbeams, beckoning rare.

Shadows dance in silver light,
Veiling secrets born from night.
Nature's canvas, cold and bright,
Unveils wonders in twilight's flight.

A tapestry of dreams afloat,
In frozen droplets, thoughts we note.
Frost-kissed wonders guide our way,
Through secret paths where shadows play.

Chill of the Unspoken Night

The moon hangs high, a silent guide,
Whispers of wind in shadows hide.
Stars twinkle soft, a distant light,
Embracing all in the chill of night.

Branches sway with a ghostly grace,
Crickets hush in this tranquil space.
The world holds breath, time seems to freeze,
In secret corners, a gentle breeze.

Footsteps muffled on soft, white snow,
Echoes linger, then gently go.
A night so still, it draws us near,
In the unspoken, whispers clear.

Dreams take flight on the frosty air,
Sharing secrets we long to share.
The chill brings warmth to souls exposed,
In the night's embrace, we find repose.

Serene Landscapes Frozen in Time

Mountains rise with a timeless grace,
Blanketed white, they silently face.
A tranquil lake, a reflecting glass,
Frozen whispers in the moments that pass.

Trees stand tall, their branches adorned,
Nature waits, in stillness reborn.
Footprints trace where stories unfold,
In serene landscapes, mysteries told.

Rivers slow under winter's reign,
Glacial art in a quiet domain.
Each breath a cloud, each sigh a song,
Time stretches wide, where hearts belong.

The beauty lingers, quietly vast,
Reminding us of the beauty past.
In this frozen scene, peace does climb,
In serene landscapes, frozen in time.

Murmurs of the Frosted Ground

Underneath a blanket of white,
The earth beneath holds secrets tight.
Murmurs soft, where squirrels scurry,
Beneath the frost, there's no hurry.

Every leaf, a story untold,
In stillness, nature's charm unfolds.
Brittle twigs in the twilight gleam,
Whispers dance like a half-formed dream.

The gentle crunch beneath my toes,
In the quiet, a magic grows.
Winter's breath wraps the world in art,
Murmurs echo, a beating heart.

Nature listens in tranquil peace,
All melodies and echoes cease.
In frosted realms where silence binds,
We hear the stories of freeze-framed times.

The Unseen Artistry of Winter

Moments captured, pure and bright,
Winter weaves with unseen light.
Frosty breath on a window pane,
Artistry forms in nature's reign.

Icicles like diamonds hang,
In every branch, a song is sang.
Winds carve shapes in snow and air,
Winter's hand is both bold and rare.

Each flake a marvel, unique and fine,
In silent galleries, they align.
A canvas wide, in hushed delight,
The unseen artistry of night.

Colors muted, yet deeply felt,
In winter's grasp, our hearts are knelt.
Embraced by cold, we find the heat,
In the unseen, our spirits meet.

Glacial Moments of Midnight Solitude

Underneath the blanket of night,
Stars whisper secrets, trimmed in light.
Silence wraps the world in calm,
Embracing dreams, a soothing balm.

Frozen breath dances on the air,
Time pauses still, devoid of care.
Moonlit shadows paint the ground,
In this stillness, peace is found.

Crickets sing their lullaby,
Beneath the vast, unyielding sky.
Glacial moments stretch the frame,
Eternity, a silent name.

Nature's breath hangs like a pearl,
In these pauses, memories swirl.
Fragile ice in the quiet night,
Holds time gently in its light.

Here, the heart finds time to roam,
In glacial stillness, we feel at home.
Each moment a fleeting embrace,
In midnight's depth, we find our place.

Fleeting Reflections in Icy Ponds

Gentle ripples break the glass,
Mirrored worlds that flicker past.
Beneath the surface, dreams reside,
Where fleeting thoughts and wishes hide.

Whispers of the wind float by,
Carried forth on a breathy sigh.
Stars twinkle in the pool's embrace,
As shadows dance in frozen space.

Cold stillness holds the evening tight,
Capturing every day's last light.
Ponds echo tales of what has been,
In chilly depths, life's mysteries spin.

Reflections shiver, fade away,
Like fleeting thoughts that stray and sway.
In icy waters, stories dwell,
Each one a secret, time will tell.

So let us linger by this shore,
Where fleeting moments promise more.
In icy ponds, our hopes unfold,
Like tales of warmth from winters cold.

Midnight's Embrace of Stillness

In the midst of midnight's glow,
A quiet whisper soft and slow.
The world beneath a velvet dome,
Here in stillness, hearts find home.

Frosted trees stand tall and proud,
Wrapped in silence, wrapped in shroud.
Moonbeams kiss the sleeping ground,
In midnight's realm, calm is profound.

Gentle shadows weave their tale,
In the night where dreams set sail.
Stars blink softly, a secret song,
Carried in the night, where we belong.

Every heartbeat seems to pause,
Grasping at the quiet cause.
Midnight's embrace holds time so dear,
In its silence, all feels clear.

Here, under the sky so wide,
In stillness, we can safely glide.
Wrapped in peace, away from strife,
Midnight's embrace, the gift of life.

Enchanted by the Frosty Glow

A frosty glow blankets the trees,
Whispers of magic carried by the breeze.
Snowflakes twirl in the moonlit air,
Painting the night with a soft, white flair.

Each breath a mist, a fleeting trace,
In this enchanted, winter place.
Stars hang bright with gentle grace,
Illuminating this sacred space.

The world, a canvas of crystal gems,
Nature's art where wonder stems.
Underneath the frost-covered skies,
We find the beauty that never dies.

In quiet moments, we pause and gaze,
Caught in the winter's wondrous daze.
Each soft flake tells a story true,
Of beauty born from the icy blue.

As night unfolds with a shimmering glow,
We're enchanted, wrapped in winter's flow.
Amidst the chill, our hearts do swell,
For in this magic, all is well.

Frosted Whispers Beneath the Stars

In the quiet night sky, they twinkle bright,
A dance of dreams in the pale moonlight.
Frosted whispers float through the air,
Secrets of winter, tender and rare.

Each breath a crystal, crisp and clear,
Silent stories only the stars hear.
Beneath the blanket of glistening white,
Hope glimmers softly, a beautiful sight.

With every flutter, the snowflakes share,
The magic of moments, precious and rare.
Under the dome where the shadows play,
Frosted whispers guide hearts on their way.

In this enchanted realm, time stands still,
The night envelops with gentle thrill.
A tapestry woven of silver and blue,
Frosted whispers beckon, inviting anew.

Shimmering Stillness of the Night

Stars drip like jewels on a velvet spread,
Embracing the silence, where dreams dare tread.
The moon casts a glow, soft and divine,
In shimmering stillness, our hearts intertwine.

Wisps of the breeze carry stories untold,
In the hush of the night, both tender and bold.
Crickets serenade the end of the day,
As shadows dance lightly, in playful sway.

Beneath the vast sky, we breathe in deep,
Finding solace in stillness, where secrets seep.
The world fades away, with every soft sigh,
In shimmering stillness, together we lie.

A moment suspended, eternal and bright,
Cradled in wonder, until morning's light.
With stars in our eyes, we linger and dream,
In the shimmering stillness, life feels supreme.

Muffled Footsteps on Ice

In a world wrapped in white, we tread so light,
Muffled footsteps echo in the still of the night.
Each step a whisper against the cold ground,
As frosted breath dances, soft and profound.

Crystalline beauty sparkles all around,
With every small movement, a delicate sound.
Beneath our weary soles, the secrets lie,
Muffled footsteps trace where shadows sigh.

The landscape calls softly, a siren's song,
Guiding our hearts as we wander along.
Through the silence, a promise of peace,
Muffled footsteps whisper, inviting release.

Every crackle of ice, a story begins,
Written in frost where the chill gently spins.
We carry the echoes, a memory's trace,
Muffled footsteps lead us to a sacred space.

Serene Shroud of Silver

Under the blanket of a silver embrace,
The world rests softly, a tranquil place.
Moonlight spills gently, like dreams in the night,
In the serene shroud, everything feels right.

Branches adorned with a delicate hue,
Whispering secrets known only to few.
The stillness surrounds, a cradle of calm,
Lending the night a soothing balm.

In the hush of the evening, hearts open wide,
Wrapped in the magic that winter provides.
Each sigh a melody, soft as a dove,
In the serene shroud of silver, we love.

Stars mingle softly in the cool, crisp air,
Painting the canvas with beauty so rare.
With every heartbeat, we feel so alive,
In the serene shroud of silver, we thrive.

The Peace of a Sunlight-Blanketed Frost

Morning sun touches the frost,
Glimmers sparkle, nature's gloss.
Soft whispers fill the chilled air,
A world wrapped in beauty so rare.

Branches wear coats made of white,
Shadows dance in the soft light.
Each blade of grass, a crystal star,
Miracles bloom, both near and far.

Silence speaks through the trees,
Carried gently by the breeze.
Heartbeats slow in the quiet glow,
Underneath the sun's warm throw.

Nature hums a soothing tune,
Crafted by the rising moon.
Laughter echoing off the glade,
In moments shared, fears start to fade.

Frost retreats, surrendering grace,
To the golden sun's embrace.
In this peace, we find our way,
A perfect end to winter's sway.

Echoes of Soft Chill Across the Landscape

Cold dawn settles on the field,
Nature wraps her arms, concealed.
Footsteps crunch on frosty ground,
In stillness, wonders can be found.

Colors muted, whispers low,
Frozen streams begin to flow.
Birdsongs echo, thick with air,
A gentle moment, we all share.

Trees stand tall in quietude,
Nature calls us to her mood.
Gentle flakes begin to fall,
In their dance, we hear the call.

Breath visible in the mist,
Every flicker, a moment kissed.
Frosty breath in the morning light,
Each heartbeat echoes, pure delight.

Soft chill lingers, a warm embrace,
In this stillness, time finds grace.
Beneath the surface, life is true,
Awake and waiting, reaching through.

Drifting Thoughts Amidst Hazy White

Hazy clouds blanket the gray sky,
Thoughts drift slowly, like birds that fly.
Meadow glistens with soft white sheen,
In the stillness, all feels serene.

Whispers caught in frosty air,
Breezes dance without a care.
Moments pause as time unspools,
Wrapped in nature's gentle rules.

Snowflakes fall in playful whirl,
Like tiny ships on a world unfurl.
Each gust carries fluffy dreams,
In silence, our soul redeems.

Footprints lead where time may flow,
Through the woods where magic grows.
Each path taken is softly spun,
Connecting hearts, we're all as one.

Drifting thoughts, a winter's day,
In this quiet, we softly sway.
With every breath, we find our peace,
Nature's canvas, a sweet release.

The Serenity of Nature's Pause

A moment graced by nature's hand,
Whispers echo across the land.
Time stands still in tranquil ways,
Serenity found in soft displays.

Clouds drift slowly, shadows play,
Gentle colors kiss the day.
Mountains stand in silence proud,
Wrapped in peace, a gentle shroud.

Rippling streams, a soothing sound,
Nature's heartbeat all around.
In the quiet, dreams awake,
Moments held as memories make.

Leaves rustle in the soft wind,
Stories beckon from within.
Underneath the endless sky,
Hearts connect with every sigh.

The world's embrace, a soft retreat,
In each pause, our lives complete.
Harmony swells, love's gentle song,
In nature's arms, we all belong.

Silent Crystals at Dawn

The morning breaks with quiet light,
Silent crystals shimmer bright.
In the stillness, beauty gleams,
Nature whispers secret dreams.

Frosty patterns lace the grass,
Every moment fleeting, fast.
Birds awaken, soft and small,
Echoes of a gentle call.

Sunlight kisses the cold ground,
In its warmth, new life is found.
Each crystal, now a fading spark,
Awakens all from winter's dark.

As the day unfolds its grace,
Softly falls the night's embrace.
Silence reigns as stars appear,
Crystals glisten, night is near.

In the twilight, dreams take flight,
Silent whispers, pure delight.
Nature's beauty, calm and drawn,
Forever found in silent dawn.

Whispering Winter's Embrace

Snowflakes dance on the chilly air,
Whispers soft, they swirl and tear.
In the stillness, secrets sigh,
Winter's breath is low and shy.

Trees adorned with shimmering white,
Branches glisten in soft twilight.
Footprints left by passersby,
A fleeting moment, passing by.

Fires crackle in cozy rooms,
Laughter mingles, joy resumes.
Wrapped in warmth with hearts that race,
Together, find a safe embrace.

Frosty windows framed in lace,
Nature's artwork finds its place.
Through the chill, a tender hold,
Whispers echo, stories told.

When the sun begins to rise,
Winter's grip will softly die.
Yet the echoes will remain,
In our hearts, a gentle pain.

The Lullaby of Frozen Leaves

In the woods where silence sleeps,
Frozen leaves in slumber keep.
Crystals blanket every bough,
Nature's lullaby sings low.

Gentle breezes brush the trees,
Whispers carried on the freeze.
Every branch a story holds,
Winter's magic, quiet, bold.

Stars above in velvet skies,
Like diamonds in the evening's eyes.
The moonlight spills a silver sheen,
A serene, enchanted scene.

Dreams are woven through the night,
Lullabies take gentle flight.
In this stillness, hearts unite,
Softly wrapped in winter's light.

When the dawn begins to break,
Sleepy eyes will start to wake.
Yet the whispers will remain,
In the echoes of the plain.

Chill Over the Sleeping Earth

A blanket soft, the earth does wear,
Cloaked in whispers, frosty air.
Dawn approaches, cool and clear,
Breath of winter, drawing near.

Glistening fields, a tranquil sight,
Underneath, the world is white.
Every tree stands bold and tall,
Wrapped in silence, nature's call.

Clouds above in gentle gray,
Hiding sun's warm, golden ray.
Yet beneath the icy guise,
Life waits patiently to rise.

Slowly warms the chilling breath,
Renewal waits beyond the death.
Spring will come, though winters last,
In the future, shadows past.

As the seasons softly turn,
Hearts will thaw, and spirits burn.
In the chill, we find our worth,
In the quiet of the earth.

Hibernation of Sound in the Glare

In the quiet of winter's embrace,
Whispers fade in soft twilight,
Snow blankets the world in white lace,
Silence dances in the fading light.

Footsteps muffled, lost in the cold,
Echoes linger, yet are no more,
Time slows down, a tale untold,
Every moment, a gentle shore.

The sun glimmers on icy chains,
Reflecting dreams of long-lost tunes,
Frozen breaths, like delicate veins,
Softly weave through winter's swoons.

Nature rests in a crystal seam,
Colors muted, the world subdued,
In this stillness, we find a dream,
A melody of solitude.

As days blend into night's tender fold,
We listen close to the heart's own sound,
In hibernation, new tales unfold,
Where silence sings, the soul is found.

Crystal Echoes of Time Stopped

In the halls of frozen memories,
Shadows linger on ancient stone,
Time enfolds in nostalgic pleas,
In crystal echoes, we're not alone.

The air shimmers, a quiet grace,
Moments freeze like delicate glass,
In twilight's glow, we find our place,
Each heartbeat a thread, ready to pass.

Whispers carry on the winter breeze,
Ghostly notes in the pale moonlight,
A melody wrapped in the trees,
While stars blanket the depth of night.

Here, within this frozen embrace,
We dance slowly, no rush to move,
Crystalline dreams take us to a space,
Where echoes of time gently groove.

In this realm where the past collides,
We hold the present, a fleeting hour,
With every breath, the universe bides,
In crystal echoes, we find our power.

Shadows in Frost's Tight Grip

Beneath the weight of frosty breath,
Shadows stretch, entwined and bold,
Whispers of life embrace the death,
As daylight fades and night takes hold.

Trees stand bare, their secrets shared,
In moon's soft glow, they softly weep,
While starlit skies hang unprepared,
In winter's grasp, the world is deep.

Every corner, a tale of night,
Frosty fingers weave through the dark,
Shadows linger, in still delight,
Echoes whisper a ghostly spark.

In this quiet, a promise sings,
Of warmth to come when spring returns,
But for now, the chill it brings,
Holds us close as stillness churns.

The world asleep in a shrouded trance,
We find solace in frozen time,
In frost's tight grip, we take our chance,
To dance with shadows, deep and sublime.

Lofty Calm Under the Winter Sky

Beneath the vast, unyielding dome,
A tranquil hush blankets the land,
Clouds drift softly, a wandering home,
While snowflakes twirl, a gentle hand.

The air, crisp, breathes life anew,
In its silence, the heart takes flight,
Stars sprinkle silver on the blue,
As day yields softly into night.

Mountains loom in quiet might,
Capped in white, they stand so still,
In this calm, the world feels right,
A canvas vast, so pure, so real.

Owl calls from its frosty perch,
Echoing through the still of night,
Nature's peace, a sacred church,
Where dreams are woven, full of light.

In lofty calm, we breathe in deep,
With each inhale, we find our ways,
Through winter's hush, our spirits leap,
Under the stars, where hope stays.

Shimmering Stillness Under Moonlight

In the calm of night, stars gleam bright,
Silence holds the world, a gentle sight.
Whispers of dreams float on the breeze,
Wrapped in the glow of the swaying trees.

Crickets sing softly, a lullaby clear,
The moon dances low, drawing us near.
Shadows stretch long, caressed by light,
In shimmering stillness, we find our flight.

Here in this moment, time seems to freeze,
Every heartbeat echoes with perfect ease.
Thoughts unravel like ribbons of light,
In shimmering stillness, everything feels right.

A path made of silver, a river of stars,
Guides us through night, wherever we are.
The world fades away, just you and I,
In shimmering stillness, we learn to fly.

As dawn softly whispers, the sky turns gold,
Memories of night in our hearts unfold.
Though morning arrives with its warm embrace,
The shimmering stillness will always hold space.

Ethereal Breath of Crystal Air

In a realm where dreams and whispers play,
The breath of crystal carries night away.
Misty tendrils weave through ancient trees,
Dancing softly in the gentle breeze.

Moonlit ferns glisten with delicate grace,
Reflecting a world wrapped in silver lace.
Each inhaled moment, a melody rare,
Filled with the magic of crystal air.

Echoes of laughter in shadows lie still,
The air wraps around with an ethereal thrill.
With every exhale, a secret we share,
Breathe in the wonder of this crystal air.

Where time drifts slowly under starlit skies,
Dreams float like clouds where the heart never lies.
Each breath taken softly, a treasure we bear,
Lost in the beauty of ethereal air.

As dawn breaks the spell, colors renew,
The crystal fades gently, a soft adieu.
Though day claims the light, our spirits declare,
We'll return to the night for that breezy affair.

Shadows Wrapped in Winter's Embrace

In the hush of night, shadows creep near,
Winter's breath whispers, crisp and clear.
Blankets of snow cover the ground,
Softly caressing, a silence profound.

Branches stand bare, silhouetted and cold,
A tapestry woven with stories untold.
The chill in the air gives room for grace,
As shadows are wrapped in winter's embrace.

Footsteps echo where the frost has kissed,
Each moment of stillness, a fleeting bliss.
The world feels enchanted, slow as a race,
In the heart of the night, winter keeps pace.

Stars twinkle brightly, like diamonds alight,
In the arms of the moon, everything feels right.
Holding our dreams, in this fragile place,
Lost inside shadows, wrapped in winter's embrace.

When morning unfurls with a pastel hue,
The shadows retreat, bidding adieu.
Yet memories linger in every trace,
Of shadows held dear, in winter's embrace.

The Lullaby of Frosty Nights

As night descends, the world starts to rest,
Blankets of white cover nature's crest.
A lullaby sings through the trees so tall,
In frosty whispers, it beckons us all.

Moonbeams weave softly through crystalline air,
Illuminating secrets that none can compare.
With each chilly breath, the silence ignites,
In the heart of the moment, on frosty nights.

Snowflakes fall gently like dreams from the sky,
A world wrapped in wonder, as time drifts by.
The stars are our guardians, shining so bright,
Guiding our hearts through these frosty nights.

Every heartbeat dances with whispers of peace,
A serenade crafted that never shall cease.
In the cradle of darkness, our worries take flight,
Embraced by the magic of frosty night.

As dawn breaks anew, with hues warm and bold,
The lullaby fades, but the warmth we hold.
Though shadows retreat and the day takes its height,
We carry the lullaby of frosty nights.

Enchanted Stillness in the Bitter Air

In the chill of dusk, shadows play,
Whispers of snowflakes glide and sway.
Branches glisten with a sparkling sheen,
Nature's breath holds a tranquil scene.

Stars twinkle like secrets in the sky,
Echoes of silence, the world awry.
Frozen echoes of memories unfold,
Tender moments in the bitter cold.

Moonlight dances on the vaulted trees,
Caressing the night with a gentle breeze.
Dreams are woven in the crisp air's thread,
In this stillness, where all fear is shed.

The world pauses, wrapped in soft white,
Time flows slowly, lost in the night.
A hush envelops the gathering frost,
In enchanted stillness, nothing is lost.

Frostbound Stories in the Night

Frost creeps in blankets, silver and white,
Tales from the past whisper soft to the night.
Each crystal glimmers, a story untold,
Frozen reflections in the air so cold.

The moon weaves a tapestry, bright in the dark,
Illuminating truths hidden, a spark.
Under the stars, we gather near,
Sharing our stories, dissolving all fear.

The quiet of night cradles our dreams,
Rivers of thought flow in luminous streams.
In frostbound silence, we find our grace,
Time slows its march in this sacred space.

Voices of echoes dance on the breeze,
Each laugh a promise, each sigh a tease.
In the heart of winter, our bond is strong,
In the hush of the night, we belong.

With every heartbeat, the frostlands sigh,
Under the canopy of a velvet sky.
Frozen in moments, we cherish delight,
Frostbound stories cradled tight.

Veiled Dreams in a Shimmering Dawn

Morning breaks in colors bright and keen,
Veils of mist wrap the waking scene.
Whispers of dreams linger on soft lips,
As daylight unfolds, the night gently slips.

Fields shimmer like diamonds, kissed by light,
Every dewdrop a gem, twinkling, bright.
Birds sing melodies, sweet and clear,
Chasing away all the shadowed fear.

The horizon blushes in shades of gold,
Stories of hope in each sunrise told.
Embracing the warmth on our upturned face,
Veiled dreams dissolve in this sacred space.

A moment of silence, a sigh of relief,
In shimmering dawn, we find belief.
With every heartbeat, the world feels new,
In the hush of morning, aspirations brew.

Colors dance softly, a canvas divine,
Painting our futures, one stroke at a time.
In the dawn's embrace, we rise and stand tall,
Veiled dreams now vivid, answering the call.

A Whisper of Ice on Waking Hills

On waking hills, where silence reigns,
A whisper of ice flows through the plains.
Nature holds secrets beneath frosted breath,
A stillness that speaks of life and death.

Each step we take leaves a crystal trace,
In the hush of the morning's quiet grace.
Winter's soft kiss touches the ground,
As echoes of dreams flutter all around.

Hills cradle stories of seasons gone by,
With every gust of wind, we hear the sigh.
Frosted whispers weave through the trees,
Carrying tales on the biting breeze.

Branches arch gently, bowing in prayer,
Sharing their wisdom with the crisp air.
The world awakens to a chill embrace,
In ice-laden whispers, we find our place.

As the sun peeks through, warmth starts to rise,
Transforming the landscape before our eyes.
A dance of light on the glistening hills,
A whisper of ice, where magic fulfills.

The Calm Before the Thaw

The world stands still and waits,
A hush that fills the air,
Nature holds its breath tight,
In this moment, all seems fair.

Beneath a blanket, white and soft,
Dreams of spring begin to swell,
Whispers of warmth drift gently by,
Stories yet untold, they dwell.

Branches draped in crystal lace,
Glisten under morning's eye,
A fragile beauty, poised for change,
In silence, time seems to fly.

The sun stirs slowly in the sky,
Casting rays that gently glow,
Hope awakens from its sleep,
As life begins to ebb and flow.

Soon the thaw will break the spell,
Freeing all that once stood still,
Nature dances, joyously bright,
Wrapped in warmth and vibrant thrill.

A Season of Quiet Reflections

In the stillness, thoughts align,
Whispers of the heart take flight,
Each moment a chance to ponder,
Underneath the starry night.

Memories like fallen leaves,
Twirling in a gentle breeze,
Softly settling on the ground,
A treasure trove, if one sees.

Shadows stretch in evening's glow,
Silhouettes of dreams once chased,
In this quiet, solace finds,
A peace that cannot be replaced.

Eyes closed tight, visions unfold,
Journey through what was, what's now,
In a tapestry of thought,
Threads of life, a sacred vow.

The soul speaks in silent tones,
Revelations born from rest,
A season of profound insight,
In stillness, we are truly blessed.

Delicate Crystals in the First Light

Morning breaks with tender grace,
Crystals glimmer on the ground,
A world dressed in diamond hues,
Nature's jewels shining round.

Frosty breath of winter whispers,
Softly wrapping every tree,
In this gleam, all things awake,
As if life's a symphony.

The sun peeks through the icy veil,
Casting light on glistening trails,
Hope dances on the surface,
As warmth begins to unveil.

Each crystal holds a story dear,
Of nights when stars did glow bright,
Now, as dawn rises anew,
They reflect the morning light.

A fragile beauty sets the stage,
For the bloom of life to thrive,
In delicate crystals, magic,
Reminds us all, we are alive.

Luminescence of a Frigid Moon

Beneath a sky of velvet blue,
A frigid moon begins to rise,
Casting shadows on the snow,
A beacon bright, a wise disguise.

Chilled winds sing a haunting tune,
As night unfolds its mystic charms,
Wrapped in calm, the world holds tight,
To the moon's enchanting arms.

Each star whispers secrets old,
In the quiet, dreams ignite,
A tapestry of silver dreams,
Woven softly, pure delight.

The frosted earth reflects its glow,
Embracing night with open arms,
In this moment, everything's whole,
Underneath the moon's soft charms.

As time drifts slowly, gently sways,
The frigid moon begins to dance,
In luminescence, hearts take flight,
Underneath this starlit trance.

Veiled in Solitude of the Season

In shadows deep, the world is hushed,
The whispering winds, a soft, sweet brush.
Leaves flutter down, like thoughts set free,
As solitude wraps the weary tree.

Beneath the boughs, all time stands still,
Reflecting dreams on the quiet hill.
A twilight glow, where moments blend,
In silence, broken only by the bend.

Each breath of dusk, a gentle sigh,
As stars awaken in the evening sky.
Nature rests, her secrets kept,
In veiled repose, the world has slept.

The season calls, with frosty breath,
A dance of life, and whispers of death.
Crimson and gold, lost in the fray,
As solitude blooms, in its own way.

A single path through golden leaves,
Where hope ignites and heart believes.
In quietude, the spirit finds,
The beauty laced in time's designs.

Ghostly Breath in Fading Light

Whispers crawl through the dusky air,
As shadows stretch, life lays bare.
Ghostly echoes dance in flight,
In the fading glow of gentle light.

The horizon bleeds in hues of gray,
Lost moments drift, then float away.
Each breath of twilight breathes a sigh,
Leaving soft trails as night draws nigh.

Familiar shapes now twist and wane,
Memories linger like a soft refrain.
A spectral glow wraps the weary soul,
In the fading light, we feel whole.

With every turn, the dark unfolds,
Stories whispered, secrets told.
A tapestry woven of dreams and fears,
In the ghostly dusk, we shed our tears.

Time unravels like fog in flight,
Under the watch of the silver night.
In this embrace, we find our grace,
In fading light, we find our place.

Nature's Still Heartbeat in Winter

Under blankets of glistening white,
Nature sleeps, embraced by night.
The world holds its breath, so calm, so pure,
In winter's arms, we find allure.

Frosted branches, a stunning sight,
With whispers of peace, the air feels right.
A quietude reigns, soft and sweet,
In nature's pause, our hearts repeat.

Footprints trace in fresh, soft snow,
A silent path where dreams can grow.
Each flake a miracle, crafted with care,
Dancing down from the crisp, cold air.

Clouds drift by in a muted hue,
As sunlight weaves its golden thread through.
The world still beats with a quiet grace,
In winter's arms, we find our place.

Stories unfurl in the frosty breeze,
A melody whispered among the trees.
In the stillness here, our spirits soar,
Nature's heartbeat, forever more.

Eloquent Silence of the Snowfall

Softly falling, the snow descends,
A silent hush where music bends.
Each flake a whisper, light as air,
In eloquence, a world laid bare.

The moonlight dances on frosted ground,
In this stillness, peace is found.
Gentle drifts, a quilt so bright,
Wrap the earth in a cloak of light.

The night exhales, a breath so fine,
In every flurry, magic entwines.
Footsteps muted on this white sea,
Echo the heart's sweet reverie.

Above, the stars wink in delight,
As snowflakes twinkle against the night.
In this embrace, the world stands still,
An eloquent silence, time to fill.

From the quiet depth, stories arise,
Painting the canvas of endless skies.
In this wintry spell, we find our way,
In eloquent silence, night turns to day.

The Hush of Waking Grass

In morning light, the dew is bright,
A carpet green, so fresh and light.
Each blade awakes, with gentle grace,
A quiet world, a sacred space.

Whispers dance on soft, cool air,
Nature stirs with tender care.
Beneath the sky, so vast and blue,
The hush of grass, a world anew.

Beams of sun, they weave and play,
Chasing shadows, night gives way.
The rustling leaves, a soft refrain,
The hush of grass, a sweet remain.

As creatures rise, their day begins,
The chorus of life softly spins.
In this calm, our spirits soar,
The hush of waking grass, we adore.

A dance of life, a tune profound,
In every corner, beauty found.
We walk amongst this grace so vast,
In harmony with nature cast.

The Winter's Breath Beneath Our Feet

Frost-kissed paths, a chilling breeze,
The world adorned in winter's ease.
Each step we take, a crunching sound,
The winter's breath, a dance profound.

Blankets white, where silence reigns,
Whispers of cold in window panes.
The trees stand tall, their branches bare,
The winter's breath, a frosty air.

Through icy fields, we wander brave,
In nature's grasp, we feel its wave.
The crispness bites, yet warms the heart,
The winter's breath, a fleeting art.

As twilight falls, the sky ignites,
Stars emerge in chilly nights.
With every step, we share its song,
The winter's breath, where we belong.

In stillness found, the world transforms,
Embracing cold as beauty warms.
With every footfall, life we greet,
The winter's breath beneath our feet.

Silvery Threads of a Gentle Sleep

The moonlight weaves a silken strand,
A lullaby from dreamland's hand.
In shadows deep, the whispers twine,
Silvery threads, a night divine.

Each star a note in silenced tune,
As night enfolds beneath the moon.
Wrapped in soft, eternal peace,
Silvery threads, the heart's release.

The world drifts off, a fleeting sigh,
In tranquil arms, we gently lie.
With dreams that soar on wings of light,
Silvery threads, our guiding night.

In slumber deep, our worries cease,
A tapestry of sweet increase.
With visions bright, we softly creep,
On silvery threads of a gentle sleep.

Awake we rise, to greet the dawn,
Yet still we feel the night's soft yawn.
In morning's glow, we'll carry deep,
The silvery threads of a gentle sleep.

Impressions Left by the Cool Touch

With each caress, a whisper cool,
Nature's hand, a gentle tool.
The breeze that flows through branches high,
Leaves impressions as it sweeps by.

On dewy morns, the earth feels sweet,
A cool embrace beneath our feet.
The scents of pine, the damp of moss,
Impressions left, no moments lost.

As shadows stretch and sunlight fades,
Cool touches linger in the glades.
In twilight's glow, we pause to breathe,
Impressions left by what we perceive.

Each rustling leaf, a story told,
In temperatures both warm and cold.
The world around, each detail such,
Impressions left by the cool touch.

In memory's garden, we walk slow,
With every step, the feelings grow.
In nature's arms, we feel the crutch,
Impressions left by the cool touch.

Dreams Woven in the Frosted Air

In the twilight glow, whispers call,
Snowflakes twirl, through branches tall.
Silvery threads of a world unseen,
We weave our dreams in the frosty sheen.

Each breath a mist in the crisp night,
Stars above, a shimmering sight.
Echoes dance on the chilly breeze,
In frosted air, our hearts find ease.

We trace our wishes on the snow,
With every step, our hopes aglow.
In quiet moments, the magic starts,
As winter cradles our longing hearts.

The moonlight kisses each icy crest,
A gentle hush, nature's rest.
In dreams woven tight with silver thread,
We chase the night till the stars have fled.

Awake to find this morning bright,
The day unfurls in softest light.
With dreams embraced by the frosty air,
We carry wonder, and love to share.

Shy Embraces of Winter's Grasp

In quiet corners where shadows dance,
Winter whispers with a fleeting chance.
Trees stand tall, draped in white lace,
Nature's beauty, a shy embrace.

The chill wraps round like a gentle sigh,
Breath like smoke, as moments fly.
In this stillness, the world slows down,
A frosty crown on nature's brow.

Footprints mark where lovers tread,
In whispers soft, sweet words are said.
Beneath the frost, life still waits,
Winter's grasp, a time creates.

Snowflakes tumble, a delicate fall,
Each one unique, answering the call.
In the hush of night, let spirits blend,
As winter's arms embrace, we mend.

With every flake, we find our peace,
In snowy realms, all worries cease.
Together in the cold, we find our place,
In shy embraces of winter's grace.

The Still Heart of Nature Awaits

Beneath the blanket of purest white,
Nature rests in the still of night.
Frozen rivers, a glimmering seam,
Held in silence, a whispered dream.

The trees stand firm, cloaked in frost,
In this stillness, we count the cost.
Yet life is brewing beneath the ground,
In Nature's heart, all secrets abound.

Gentle winds carry tales of old,
Whispers of warmth, a promise bold.
With every breath, the earth holds fast,
In slumber deep, till spring is cast.

Crystals shimmer in the pale dawn light,
Reflecting hope in each fairy bright.
The still heart beats in rhythm slow,
Awaiting warmth from the sun's soft glow.

In quietude, we find our song,
In Nature's arms, we all belong.
The still heart of the world abides,
And in that stillness, love resides.

Radiance in Frosty Silence

When morning breaks with chilly grace,
A quiet beauty starts to trace.
Resplendent frost on every leaf,
In chilled embrace, we find relief.

The world transformed in icy touch,
Radiance gleams, though the night is hush.
Snowy blankets veiling the earth,
In frost's embrace, there's silent mirth.

Crystal droplets hanging tight,
Sparkle bright in morning light.
In every corner, shadows play,
A masterpiece, the dawn's ballet.

Winter's breath, a gentle sigh,
Moments linger as time slips by.
In frosty silence, peace takes hold,
Within our hearts, warmth to behold.

As sunlight dances on the snow,
Life's quiet radiance starts to grow.
In every glimmer, dreams entwine,
In winter's hands, our hopes align.

The Hibernating Breath of the World

In silent woods where echoes play,
The earth wraps deep in white array.
Soft whispers drift on frosty air,
A world at rest, devoid of care.

The rivers slow, the skies grow gray,
Icicles form where children sway.
Nature holds its breath with grace,
In winter's kind, embracing lace.

The distant hills, a muted hue,
Cloaked in snow, a timeless view.
The night unfolds, stars gleam anew,
In this stillness, dreams come through.

Beneath the frost, life softly sleeps,
The promise of spring, buried deep.
Yet in this hush, hope gently stirs,
A soft reminder, life endures.

Winter's breath, a tender keep,
Cradling hearts in slumbering sweep.
Whispers of warmth begin to spread,
As winter's tale, its thread is fed.

Coated in a Blanket of Tranquility

Softly falling, flakes of white,
Gentle layers hug the night.
A tranquil world, serene and still,
In frosty air, the time does thrill.

Each branch adorned with crystal lace,
Nature finds its quiet grace.
The world wrapped tight in peace's hands,
Where silence rests and beauty stands.

Footprints print the powdery ground,
In this stillness, joy is found.
With every breath, the heart feels whole,
Winter's warmth within the soul.

A canvas vast, so pure and bright,
Underneath the cloak of night.
A world of dreams, where silence reigns,
Coated in peace, life gently wanes.

Winter's touch, both soft and grand,
In this hush, we understand.
Moments freeze, yet time aligns,
In tranquility, the heart shines.

Chilled Reveries of the Waiting Trees

In twilight's glow, the branches bare,
Stand waiting trees, a frozen stare.
Their limbs hold secrets, stories told,
In whispers soft, and spirits bold.

A frosty breath, the winter's tune,
Beneath the glow of a slivered moon.
The air is crisp, each moment breathes,
As time drifts slow, amidst the leaves.

The shadows dance, the silence roams,
In nature's grasp, these ancient homes.
Yearning for warmth, yet standing tall,
They brace themselves for spring's sweet call.

Beneath their bark, the life runs deep,
In hibernation, dreams they keep.
With each falling flake, they find their peace,
Awaiting blooms, a sweet release.

In every storm, they stand with pride,
Their patience strong, with arms spread wide.
Chilled dreams whisper in winter's breeze,
As hope returns to waiting trees.

Time Pauses in the Winter Light

Time stands still in winter's light,
A golden glow, a pure delight.
The world adorned in shimmering white,
Moments linger, hearts feel right.

Each flake a wish that softly falls,
In quiet grace, the wonder calls.
With every breath, the magic grows,
As stillness wraps the world in prose.

The sun dips low, the shadows play,
In tranquil hues of dusk's array.
Footprints mark the snow-kissed trails,
In this embrace, serenity prevails.

The night descends, the stars ignite,
A celestial dance, a wondrous sight.
Underneath the blanket of sky,
Time surrenders, letting dreams fly.

Winter's kiss, both soft and bright,
Bears the warmth of firelight.
In this fleeting, calm respite,
We cherish all, in winter's light.

The Hushed Breath of December

The world slows down in hues of gray,
As frosty winds begin to sway.
Silent whispers in the air,
A poignant chill, a moment rare.

Branches wear their coats of white,
Stars emerge, a twinkling sight.
Footprints vanish in the snow,
As time drifts soft and slow.

Candles flicker, shadows dance,
In the stillness, hearts take a chance.
Memories wrapped in warmth and light,
Guide us through the chilly night.

Voices hush with nature's call,
In the hush, we feel it all.
December's breath, a tender sigh,
Echoes softly, passing by.

As moments freeze, we find our peace,
Within the cold, our worries cease.
Each glimmering flake, a tale untold,
In December's grasp, we are consoled.

Ghostly Patterns in the Twilight

Twilight dances in shades of blue,
Shadows whisper secrets anew.
Figures blend with fading light,
Ghostly patterns roam the night.

Leaves flutter in a gentle breeze,
Echoes hum through ancient trees.
In the dusk, the spirits play,
In twilight's arms, they fade away.

Moonlight drapes the world in silk,
As stars spill forth like dreams of milk.
Phantoms twirl in night's embrace,
Tracing stories, leaving no trace.

Colors shift, a spectral show,
As daylight bids a soft hello.
In this hour, time stands still,
Ghostly whispers beckon thrill.

Through the veil, we wander free,
In twilight's bounty, we shall see.
The beauty of the shadows' art,
Awakens magic in the heart.

Frost-Kissed Memories in Shadows

Underneath the veils of frost,
We find the warmth in what is lost.
Whispers linger in the cold,
Frost-kissed tales of love retold.

Each breath a cloud, a fleeting trace,
As shadows wander, time will chase.
In this crisp air, we reflect,
On moments past we still protect.

A tapestry of ice and light,
Memories twinkle in the night.
In every spark, a laugh remains,
Frost-kissed echoes, joys and pains.

Silence hums a gentle tune,
Beneath the watchful, gleaming moon.
In shadows deep, our spirits sift,
Through frosty layers, memories lift.

Pulling forth the past we find,
A path woven in the mind.
Each frosted breath a tender plea,
For the warmth of what used to be.

Tranquil Veil of Icy Dreams

In the stillness, dreams reside,
Beneath a tranquil, icy tide.
Each snowflake holds a whispered wish,
As winter grants us moments swish.

Frozen fields stretch far and wide,
Crystals glisten, nature's pride.
A serene canvas, soft and deep,
Where secrets lie and shadows sleep.

Quiet echoes swirl and twine,
In this frosty space, we shine.
With every breath, the world retreats,
In icy dreams, our heartbeats meet.

The veil of cold wraps us tight,
Cradling hope in the quiet night.
Within this chill, we gently glide,
Finding warmth in the winter's ride.

So let us wander, hand in hand,
In this tranquil, frosty land.
For in the stillness, love will thrive,
In icy dreams, our souls alive.

Stillness Where Flowers Once Bloomed

In the fields where colors used to sing,
Silence reigns, a ghostly spring.
Petals dropped, the wind stands still,
Memories linger, time to fill.

Ghosts of fragrance fade away,
Beneath the sky's heavy gray.
Roots now clutch the barren earth,
Where once there was vibrant mirth.

A breeze whispers tales of old,
Forlorn stories softly told.
Nature holds its breath so deep,
In this silence where dreams sleep.

Crumbling paths in shades of brown,
Echoes of a once bright crown.
The sun retreats with gentle grace,
Leaving shadows to embrace.

Yet in stillness, hope may rise,
Beneath the muted azure skies.
Awaiting spring's warm, tender kiss,
To awaken life from its abyss.

Breath of Glacial Dreams

In the stillness, icebergs sigh,
Underneath the vast blue sky.
Frozen whispers, secrets glowed,
Tales of ages coolly flowed.

A world caught in a crystal spell,
Where time moves slow, and silence dwells.
Each breath a chill, each heartbeat light,
Amidst the frost, day meets night.

Glistening cliffs, the horizon bends,
Nature's canvas never ends.
A dance of shadows, bright and pale,
Stories captured in icy veil.

Underneath the surface, warmth hides,
Like a dream where hope abides.
With every inch, the glacier waits,
For spring to unlock celestial gates.

Snowflakes cradle the unheard song,
Of secrets kept, a journey long.
In dreams we glide, our spirits soar,
On glacial waves, forevermore.

Snowflakes Dance in Whispers

In the hush of winter's kiss,
Snowflakes twirl in quiet bliss.
Each a whisper, soft and bright,
Falling gently, pure as light.

They spiral down like fleeting dreams,
Softly weaving silver seams.
A flurry stirs the evening air,
Delicate waltz, so light, so rare.

Blankets soft on earth's embrace,
Transforming every hidden place.
Laughter echoes, pure delight,
In the dance of black and white.

Underneath the moon's soft beam,
Nature hums a gentle theme.
Twinkling stars above us gaze,
As snowflakes twirl in quiet praise.

In each flake, a story spun,
Of frosty nights, and morning sun.
They carry dreams from skies so high,
In the magic, we can fly.

Tranquil Silence Beneath a Shroud

Beneath the cloud's soft, weighty shroud,
Lies a peace, unspoken, loud.
Echoes hush with tender grace,
In this calm, we find our place.

The world outside is still and clear,
Nature whispers, drawing near.
Draped in quiet, hearts align,
Finding solace, pure, divine.

Mist rolls in, a gentle breath,
Carrying whispers of death.
Yet in the gloom, life's pulse remains,
Underneath its soft refrains.

A moment's pause, time seems to freeze,
In the stillness, a hidden breeze.
Crickets hum a low refrain,
As shadows stretch across the plain.

Here we dwell, in silent song,
A refuge where our souls belong.
Enveloped in a soft embrace,
We hold still in this sacred space.

Celestial Frost on Sleepy Pastures

A shimmering veil on gentle plains,
Stars whisper secrets in frosty chains.
The earth wears pearls, a delicate gown,
While night's soft breath slows the world down.

Colors muted, as shadows creep,
In twilight's cradle, the silence deep.
Crickets hush, the owls take flight,
As dreams arise in the heart of night.

Glistening flakes dance in the breeze,
Kissing the grass, like tender leaves.
Nature's canvas, pure and bright,
Embraced by the magic of starlit night.

Moonbeams play on the tranquil field,
While frost draws a secret shield.
Whispers of winter color the skies,
In this tranquil realm where beauty lies.

The day sleeps tight, wrapped in peace,
As frozen moments never cease.
Each breath of air holds tales untold,
In celestial frost, life's wonders unfold.

The Elegance of a Moonlit Frost

Upon the world falls a silver sheen,
Nature's beauty, calm and serene.
Moonlit whispers through frosty trees,
Tickling the night with a gentle freeze.

The rooftops glisten, each shingle bright,
Draped in the magic of soft moonlight.
Reflections dance in the still of the lake,
Each ripple curls like a lover's wake.

Frost-kissed petals in gardens sleep,
Holding the dreams that winter keeps.
An elegance wrapped in chilly grace,
Where shadows linger, and time slows its pace.

Beneath the vast and radiant sky,
The earth sighs softly, a lullaby.
Stars nod in tune, as if they know,
The beauty born in the frost's soft glow.

In this silent waltz of icy lace,
Nature reveals her timeless face.
Wrapped in the stillness, we find our place,
In the elegance of the moonlit space.

Dreamscapes Adrift in Hushed Radiance

Awake in dreams, where shadows play,
Hushed whispers cradle the end of day.
Soft glimmers wash over fields so vast,
Frosted horizons where memories last.

Colors fade into shades of blue,
In realms where wishes can come true.
Chill in the air, a soothing balm,
Nature's embrace, serene and calm.

Adrift in stillness, thoughts take flight,
Wrapped in the arms of tender night.
Each twinkling star a silent guide,
Through dreamscapes where secrets abide.

The frost unravels tales of old,
In whispered breezes, carefully told.
Moments suspended, forever remain,
In the canvas of frost, love's sweet refrain.

Glistening trails of the night's own grace,
Embrace the beauty that time can't erase.
In quiet radiance, we weave and weave,
Our dreams, unbound, where we believe.

The Stillness Wrapped in Frigid Air

Embers fade as night unfolds,
The world enshrined in silver folds.
Frozen breath drifts in silent flight,
Wrapped in stillness, bathed in night.

A crystal blanket adorns the ground,
Nature's lullaby, a gentle sound.
Stars twinkle softly, like distant fire,
In the peaceful hush, we aspire.

Branches dip low, draped in white,
As frost brings dreams to the heart of night.
Quiet moments, serene and rare,
The stillness lingers, drenched in air.

Every corner whispers tales untold,
Secrets of winter in silence unfold.
Breath visible, a clouded sigh,
In this frigid air, we gently lie.

Under the watch of the patient moon,
Time stands still, a tender boon.
Wrapped in the cold, yet warm inside,
In the stillness where our hopes reside.

Hushed Secrets Under Winter's Blanket

Whispers roam in the silent night,
Snowflakes gather, soft and white.
Beneath the layers, dreams are spun,
Silent hopes in the winter's run.

Branches bow under their weight,
Crystals glimmer, holding fate.
Each breath curls into the chill,
A moment paused, time stands still.

Beneath the stars, a tranquil sight,
The world is wrapped in soft twilight.
Footsteps hush on the frosted ground,
In winter's embrace, peace is found.

Secrets linger where shadows creep,
In the stillness, memories seep.
Frozen tales of yesteryears,
Whispered softly, lost in tears.

Underneath the icy dome,
Silent hearts find their way home.
In the quiet, love is near,
Wrapped in whispers, crystal clear.

Still Waters Reflecting the Frost

Still waters cloaked in a silver hue,
Mirror the sky, painted in blue.
Frosted edges softly gleam,
Nature echoes a frozen dream.

Ripples hush under the night,
Secret depths hidden from sight.
Whispers resonate with a sigh,
As winter stars hang low in the sky.

Reflections dance on the glassy floor,
Silent stories, forevermore.
In the stillness, time unfolds,
The beauty of winter gently holds.

When the moon casts its silver glance,
Even the shadows find their chance.
A canvas drawn by gentle hands,
Where peace and serenity takes its stands.

Echoes of frost, a gentle call,
Nature breathes, inviting all.
Still waters, a tranquil sigh,
Embrace the stillness, let it lie.

Frozen Whispers on Winter's Doorstep

Winter's breath upon the night,
Frozen whispers, soft and light.
At the threshold, secrets wait,
Wrapped in silence, marked by fate.

Footprints vanish in the snow,
Traces of where the heart must go.
Each still moment, a fleeting grace,
Held by time in a soft embrace.

Branches clothe in crystal lace,
Nature's jewelry, a stunning face.
Songs of frost in a muted sound,
In frozen echoes, peace is found.

Gathering clouds on the verge of sleep,
Tales of winter that shadows keep.
The door to dreams creaks open wide,
As night and hope gently collide.

In every corner, a story sighs,
While the world beneath the blanket lies.
Listen closely, hear the call,
Frozen whispers, enchant us all.

The Invisibility of Quietude

In the hush of early dawn,
Where silence casts a gentle pawn.
Time stands still, a breath in between,
Life unfolds in shades unseen.

In every sigh, a world awaits,
In quietude, the heart resonates.
Moments linger without a sound,
In the shadows, peace is found.

Soft as feathers, air is deep,
A tranquil promise, secrets keep.
In stillness, thoughts take flight,
As dreams emerge from the veil of night.

The weight of silence softly falls,
In its presence, the spirit calls.
Listen close, for wisdom lies,
In the spaces where quiet sighs.

To dwell in stillness is truly wise,
Where heartbeats amplify, arise.
In the invisibility of ease,
We find our solace, a gentle breeze.

Stars Dusted with Whispers of Snow

In the silent night sky, they gleam,
Whispers of snow swirl in a dream.
Under the watch of twinkling light,
Silent secrets kiss the night.

Softly they fall, a shimmering grace,
Each flake a story, each dance a trace.
Beneath the stars, the world holds still,
As winter's breath bends to our will.

Crisp air carries tales of old,
Of warmth and hearts that never fold.
In white blankets, the earth is wrapped,
While gentle slumbers, softly tapped.

Stars and snow, a cosmic blend,
Whispering secrets that will not end.
In this tapestry, the dark and bright,
We find our peace in the quiet night.

So let's embrace that whispered sheen,
In the quiet night, lost and seen.
Stars and snow, a sweet duet,
In winter's cradle, our hearts beget.

Ethereal Silence

In a world wrapped in gentle fold,
Silence whispers stories untold.
The air is thick with peace divine,
Where echoes linger, gentle, fine.

Clouds drift by in shades of grey,
Memories dance and softly sway.
Beneath the quiet, dreams emerge,
In stillness deep, our hearts converge.

A moment's pause, the world can wait,
In the hush, we contemplate.
Each breath a treasure, rich and rare,
Captured softly in the air.

Time unravels, yet stands still,
In silence, we embrace the chill.
With every heartbeat, shadows play,
In the space where night meets day.

Ethereal silence, soft and clear,
Wraps us close, alleviates fear.
In whispers low, the universe sings,
In stillness deep, our soul takes wings.

Illuminated

A splash of gold on twilight's edge,
Light dances softly, a fleeting pledge.
Through branches bare, the sunlight streams,
Awakening our silent dreams.

With every ray, a spirit lifts,
Colors bloom in nature's gifts.
In the glow, shadows bite and twist,
Moments linger, not to be missed.

In every hue, a story's spun,
Of battles lost and victories won.
Through open fields, the light does tread,
Kissing the earth where life once bled.

Support and warmth in every beam,
Uniting hearts in a radiant team.
The world illuminated, alive, aglow,
In every heart, a gentle flow.

Together we bask in this embrace,
Finding solace in the light's grace.
Illuminated paths we trod,
In every step, feeling the nod.

The Soft Melodies of Winter's Air

In winter's breath, a tranquil song,
A symphony where we belong.
With each cold gust, whispers play,
Soft melodies of the frozen day.

Snowflakes dance on crystal streams,
Cascading softly, weaving dreams.
In the chill, warmth finds a way,
Binding hearts in a gentle sway.

The world transformed in white attire,
Fires crackle, hearts inspire.
With every note, a story told,
Of warmth and love against the cold.

Nature sings in hushed refrain,
In every flake, a sweet domain.
The air is rich, a lullaby,
Beneath the vast, embracing sky.

So let us breathe this soft embrace,
In winter's song, we find our place.
Melodies drift on the frosty air,
In serene silence, love laid bare.

Echoes of Slumber in Silver Light

Beneath the moon's soft silver glow,
Dreams awaken, ebb and flow.
In whispered tones, the shadows creep,
Calling softly, lulled to sleep.

The world in quiet, hushes low,
As starlight dances, deep and slow.
Even the night wears a gentle veil,
Where echoes linger, soft and frail.

Within the silence, secrets thrive,
In silver light, we feel alive.
Each gentle breath, a tender sigh,
In whispered dreams, we silently fly.

Night wraps the earth in calming grace,
In slumber's arms, we find our place.
Every heartbeat, a soothing tune,
Guiding us gently, beneath the moon.

Echoes of dreams on the night air ride,
In silver light, our hearts confide.
So hold this moment, embrace the night,
In slumber's safety, we find our light.

Wordless Conversations in Crystal

In the hush of dawn's embrace,
Whispers dance on the cool air,
Crystal thoughts take gentle shape,
Beneath the watchful trees' stare.

Silent eyes meet, hearts align,
In the gleam of morning light,
Unseen stories intertwine,
Creating magic out of sight.

Frosted breath in the breeze,
Soft glimmers on every leaf,
Moments feel like timeless ease,
Joyful silence, pure belief.

Nature sighs in perfect peace,
Each leaf a page of soft lore,
Inviting the soul's release,
Opening wide the heart's door.

Glistening hope in every glance,
Starlit dreams in quiet dance,
In this realm, we take our chance,
With wordless love, we enhance.

Soft Glimmers Amidst the Darkness

Beneath the blanket of night sky,
Soft stars twinkle, shy and bright,
Through shadows, whispers softly sigh,
Hope flickers in the heart's light.

Each moment a glimmer, a spark,
Guiding lost souls through despair,
With warmth to ignite the dark,
Inviting peace to linger there.

Gentle breezes carry dreams,
Through the trees where shadows dance,
With moonlit paths and silver beams,
A chance for love to take a chance.

In the quiet, secrets hum,
Quiet strength in love's embrace,
In the night, soft glimmers come,
Painting shadows with pure grace.

Hope's caress through silent night,
Radiates in every heart,
In darkness, a gentle light,
Soft glimmers, a brand new start.

Echoes of Frost on the Breeze

Frosted whispers through the trees,
Echoes dance on winter's breath,
A symphony in the freeze,
Crystalline notes, life and death.

Branches twinkle, icy lace,
As twilight wraps the land in light,
Every moment, nature's grace,
Echoing soft through the night.

Chilled air carries a sweet sound,
Of memories kissed by the frost,
In this hush, our dreams are found,
With every echo, life embossed.

Night unveils its jeweled crown,
Stars are sparkling, bold and bright,
In dreams we won't lose or drown,
Each echo holds a love's light.

So let us gather, hearts in tune,
Embrace the chill in the air,
Trust the past, embrace the moon,
As echoes weave our sweet care.

Luminous Silence of Winter's Kiss

In the stillness of the night,
Winter kisses with a glow,
A hush blankets all in white,
Frosted trails of soft, slow flow.

Each flake a whisper, so divine,
Drifting softly, smooth descent,
Nature's canvas, pure and fine,
In silence, beauty is spent.

With each breath, the world stands still,
Moments stretch in crystal air,
Frozen echoes, a gentle thrill,
Warmth wrapped in winter's fair care.

Hearts align beneath the stars,
Wrapped in dreams, lost in the mist,
Time will melt all our scars,
In this silence, love persists.

So let us wander, side by side,
Through the luminous glow we find,
In winter's kiss, love will abide,
A timeless bond, gently refined.

Whispers of Winter's Kiss

Snowflakes dance in gentle flight,
Carpeting the world in white.
A breath of cold, a hush so deep,
Nature's secrets softly keep.

Bare branches reach for skies of gray,
As winter claims the fading day.
Each whisper wraps the earth in calm,
A frosty touch, a velvet balm.

Icicles hang like daggers fine,
Glimmers caught in fragile line.
The air is crisp, the silence strong,
In this stillness, we belong.

Footsteps crunch on icy ground,
Echoes of a world profound.
Winter's breath is soft and sweet,
In its arms, we find retreat.

Under moon's watch, shadows play,
Whispers flicker, fade away.
In the night, the stars ignite,
Winter's kiss, a pure delight.

Silent Chill Among the Pines

The pines stand tall, in silence bound,
A blanket deep upon the ground.
Whispers flow through crisp, cool air,
In the stillness, nothing's bare.

Frosted needles catch the light,
Glinting softly, pure and bright.
A chill winds through the winter scene,
Nature rests, serene and clean.

Beneath the boughs, the shadows grow,
Silent secrets held below.
The cold wraps tight, a soothing shawl,
In the quiet, we heed its call.

As daylight fades, a hush descends,
Winter's magic never ends.
Among the pines, we find our peace,
From the chill, our thoughts release.

Stars peek through the darkened veil,
In this moment, hearts unveil.
Silent night with dreams to sow,
Among the pines, together we go.

Frosted Veil of Dawn

Early light breaks through the haze,
A frost-clad world begins to blaze.
With each ray, the chill retreats,
Nature stirs and softly greets.

The white-tipped grass glimmers bright,
Wrapped in diamonds, pure delight.
As shadows stretch, they bid adieu,
Awakening brings colors new.

Birds begin their morning song,
In the dawn where we belong.
Frosted veils around us dance,
A fleeting moment, a sweet chance.

Pinks and golds adorn the skies,
As the daybreak softly sighs.
In this hush, our hearts align,
To the rhythm, pure divine.

Nature breathes, a sacred pause,
In this beauty without cause.
With each dawn, new echoes play,
Frosted veil, the start of day.

Hushed Echoes of Icy Morn

A glimmer of frost coats the dawn,
In the hush, the world is drawn.
Every crystal tells a tale,
Of winters past and whispers pale.

The air is sharp, a gentle bite,
Naked trees stand in pure white light.
Footsteps soft on powdery snow,
In the calm, our spirits grow.

Birds take flight in feathered arcs,
Tracing paths where beauty sparks.
Echoes linger, soft and low,
In the heart of winter's glow.

With each breath, the world transforms,
Silent magic, beauty warms.
In the stillness, time stands still,
Chasing dreams on winter's hill.

As morning breaks, the cold recalls,
Hushed echoes in nature's thralls.
In every breath, a story born,
Within the hush of icy morn.

Milton Keynes UK
Ingram Content Group UK Ltd.
UKHW010230111224
452348UK00011B/632